Infantry Soldiers

By James Nixon

CRABTREE
Publishing Company
www.crabtreebooks.com

The World's MOST DANGEROUS Jobs

Author: James Nixon
Managing editor: Paul Humphrey
Editorial director: Kathy Middleton
Editor: Adrianna Morganelli
Proofreader: Rachel Eagen
Series Design: Elaine Wilkinson
Page Design: sprout.uk.com
Cover design: Margaret Salter
Production coordinator: Margaret Salter
Prepress technician: Margaret Salter
Print coordinator: Katherine Berti

Photo credits:
J van der Wolf/Shutterstock: cover (top)
Thinkstock: Stocktrek Images:
cover (bottom)
U.S. Army: pages 5 (Sgt. Kris A. Eglin), 6
(Sgt. 1st Class SFC Horace Brown), 7 (Staff
Sgt. Michael L. Casteel), 8 (Susanne Kappler),
9 (Staff Sgt. Johnathan D. Hoover), 11 top
(Sgt. Joel Salgado), 11 bottom (Spc. Cardell
Brown), 12 (Air Force Staff Sgt. Stacy L.
Pearsall), 13 (Staff Sgt. Sean A. Foley), 14, 15
(U.S. Army Staff Sgt. Gary A. Witte), 16–17
(Sgt. 1st Class Ismael Padilla), 18 (Air Force
Staff Sgt. Stacy L. Pearsall), 19 (Petty Officer
1st Class Daniel N. Woods), 20, 21 (U.S. Army
Spc. Luther L. Boothe Jr.), 22 (Sgt. 1st Class
Andrew Kosterman), 23 (Spc. Micah E.
Clare), 24 (Ashley Strehle), 25 (Sgt. Jeffrey
Alexander), 26 (AF Staff Sgt. Brian Ferguson),
27 (Colby T. Hauser), 28, 29 (Texas Army
National Guard)

COVER STORY

◄ **COVER (top) – Dutch Army soldiers in a military vehicle in the Netherlands**

◄ **COVER (bottom) – Infantry soldiers take part in a training operation**

PAGE 1 – An infantryman fires a rocket launcher, a lightweight anti-armor weapon

Library and Archives Canada Cataloguing in Publication

Nixon, James, 1982-
    Infantry soldiers / James Nixon.

(The world's most dangerous jobs)
Includes index.
Issued also in electronic format.
ISBN 978-0-7787-5100-7 (bound).--ISBN 978-0-7787-5114-4 (pbk.)

        1. Infantry--Juvenile literature. I. Title.
II. Series: World's most dangerous jobs

UD145.N59 2012   j356'.1   C2012-901573-3

Library of Congress Cataloging-in-Publication Data

Nixon, James, 1982-
Infantry soldiers / James Nixon.
p. cm. -- (The world's most dangerous jobs)
Includes index.
Audience: Grades 4-6.
ISBN 978-0-7787-5100-7 (reinforced library binding : alk. paper) --
ISBN 978-0-7787-5114-4 (pbk. : alk. paper) -- ISBN 978-1-4271-8072-8
(electronic pdf) -- ISBN 978-1-4271-8076-6 (electronic html)
1. Soldiers--Juvenile literature. 2. Infantry--Juvenile literature. 3. Military
art and science--Juvenile literature. I. Title.

U765.N59 2012
356'.1--dc23
                                        2012008524

Crabtree Publishing Company

www.crabtreebooks.com   1-800-387-7650

Printed in Canada/042012/KR20120316

Published in Canada
Crabtree Publishing
616 Welland Ave.
St. Catharines, Ontario
L2M 5V6

Published in the United States
Crabtree Publishing
PMB 59051
350 Fifth Avenue, 59th Floor
New York, New York 10118

Published in the United Kingdom
Crabtree Publishing
Maritime House
Basin Road North, Hove
BN41 1WR

Published in Australia
Crabtree Publishing
3 Charles Street
Coburg North
VIC 3058

CONTENTS

Glossary words defined on p. 31 are in **bold** the first time they appear in the text.

INFANTRY SOLDIERS

Some people risk their lives day in, day out at work. An infantry soldier in the army carries out one of the most dangerous jobs in the world. These brave men fight enemies in combat zones around the world to protect and defend their country.

Infantry soldiers are the backbone of the army, fighting at the frontline on the ground. They close in on the enemy to kill or capture them and defend themselves when they come under fire.

Soldiers fight day and night whatever the weather, in all kinds of terrain including jungles, deserts, and mountains.

Their work is extremely dangerous and physical. They must perform hand-to-hand combat, operate weapons during battle, and remove and evade explosive devices that can kill and injure.

Troops undergo rigorous training to face the dangers of **artillery**, small arms fire, rocket attacks, and roadside bombs. Yet hundreds of soldiers are killed each year in the line of duty and many more are wounded.

"I've been an infantry soldier for four years now, and in that time I've been to Cyprus, Belize, Canada, and Afghanistan. It's amazing to think I've been to all those places in such a short space of time. I've made my best mates in the army, and I enjoy every aspect of being a soldier. You need to be fit, have a sense of humor and be ready for any challenge."

Lance Corporal McKinley, Infantry Soldier

In the race for victory, I am swift, determined, and courageous; armed with a fierce will to win. Never will I fail my country's trust… If necessary, I fight to my death.

U.S. Infantryman's Creed

DAILY DANGER

Infantry soldiers on the frontline face the threat of death and injury every day. At bases, soldiers can come under attack from gunfire and grenades. In enemy territory there is the risk of setting off deadly **mines**. Infantrymen have to constantly be on their guard.

Of all the frontline tasks undertaken by the infantry none is more risky than that of the medics. They are on the field of battle all day ready to treat any casualties. Medics put their lives in daily danger to save others.

▲ A medic cares for a soldier under fire in a field training exercise.

▶ Soldiers use their vehicles as cover during a firefight.

Specialist Bob Schumacher of the U.S. Army recently fought in the war in Iraq. Here he describes what a typical day was like:

"Every day we had a mission. It could be patrol, when we would check police stations and military checkpoints. Or we may focus on a high-value individual or target in a particular neighborhood. We could find weapons or bomb-making equipment. A lot of our intelligence comes from the Iraqis we work with. For the most part it is reliable, but it could be an ambush, so it's researched carefully before we get sent out on a mission. You can get complacent, so every time we leave it is drilled into us to pay attention and remember the danger."

A soldier fighting the insurgents in Afghanistan describes what happened when a hand grenade landed at his feet:

"I saw the grenade, and my first thought was that I knew I had to get it away from us. And my second was 'I hope this doesn't hurt too much.' As I picked it up, my thoughts were for the other guys with me - We had lost Corporal Green the day before. I didn't want to go through that again, and I wasn't prepared to see another guy from our platoon get hurt. I'd rather that it was myself than someone else. So I got my body behind the grenade and managed to throw it off."

James McKie, rifleman

TRAINING SOLDIERS

New recruits to the infantry are trained so that they are ready physically and mentally to face even the most difficult missions.

Soldiers must complete Basic Combat Training (BCT) and Advanced Individual Training (AIT) at a training school. Here, they are given a haircut and issued their army uniforms. The training starts with basic tactics followed by methods of defense against land mines and **nuclear** and chemical attacks. The soldiers are routinely tested on their fitness to ensure that they are in top physical condition.

▲ In training, soldiers practice their grenade-throwing techniques.

The infantry are then taught vital skills to give them confidence on the battlefield. They practice how to operate weapons, vehicles, and communications equipment. They learn how to prepare fighting positions and become skilled at **reconnaissance**, map reading, and **navigation**.

Advanced Individual Training is where soldiers learn to become experts in their chosen roles, whether it is a gunner, **engineer**, or medic.

Soldiers are always learning and improving. Team leaders constantly rehearse tactics, techniques, and procedures with their squads. Platoon Sergeant Curtis Reid puts a high value on making sure his soldiers are trained:

" Everyone needs training, regardless of how long they have been in. It gives our guys time to perfect these tactics that will save their lives in combat situations. Training gives soldiers the ability to perform the skills they will need under pressure. As an infantryman, you have to know how to react without thinking about it. For many of my guys, they will not realize how important that training is until a significant event occurs. "

◄ Junior soldiers work together to complete an obstacle course during a Development Training competition.

EQUIPMENT

Soldiers carry all kinds of powerful weaponry for the task of taking and holding ground. Their armory includes rifles, grenades, machine guns, and shoulder-fired rocket launchers. Fighting vehicles, such as battle tanks and heavily armored troop carriers, can drive them through the most difficult terrain.

Gunners are weapons' specialists that provide cover for troops. They fire everything from powerful machine guns to grenade launchers. Snipers are elite marksmen and some of the toughest trained in the infantry. They take out key enemy targets from hidden locations and are taught to avoid detection. **Mortar** soldiers fire explosives that hit their targets up to four miles (six km) away. Other soldiers operate missiles to take down enemy tanks and strongholds.

For protection, soldiers are equipped with helmets and state-of-the-art body armor. The infantry must also carry gas masks and protective suits in case of a chemical attack. Survival gear such as food, water, medical supplies, and ammunition is carried in pouches or rucksacks.

Extra gear may be carried depending on the mission. A personal radio allows soldiers to communicate with each other. A collapsible spade is a useful piece of equipment. It can be used to dig a defensive trench or even as a weapon.

▲ A gunner provides cover to soldiers in a firefight.

▲ A soldier takes aim with his rocket launcher.

Ranger Ryan Boyd was thankful for his body armor. He says getting shot was similar to "getting punched in the ribs 20 times in one go":

"It's an amazing bit of kit. If I hadn't had the new body armor and the side plates fitted, the round would have surely passed straight through my lungs and my heart and I probably wouldn't be here now. When I was shot it hit me in the side; it spun me right round and I ended up in the ditch on my back like a turtle."

IN BATTLE

In open battle, soldiers are at their most vulnerable. They have to control their nerves, be physically stronger, and shoot better than their opponents. Soldiers must kill the enemy before the enemy kills them.

The infantry begins an attack by firing mortars and dropping missiles on their target. The smoke created provides soldiers with cover. The infantry then moves out in **formation** to take out any enemies that have survived the bombardment. Each man keeps an eye out for enemies in their field of vision and is ready to fire.

▶ The infantry use smoke to mask their movements during battle.

As the infantry closes on its target, it splits into **flanks** to surround it. At close quarters, soldiers can use grenades or their **bayonets**. They must be careful. The enemy may have set up obstacles and booby traps, such as trip wires that set off explosives.

If soldiers come under attack they immediately return fire and find cover behind a wall or a dip in the ground. Then they aim to beat the enemy with more accurate firepower using machine guns and rifles. Terry Brazier, a gunner in the British Army, describes what happened when he came under fire in Afghanistan:

> Having located their firing positions, we suppressed the insurgents and won the fight through our heavier and more accurate fighting. We also called in a mortar strike to destroy their firing positions.
>
> Once we had won the fight we continued on our patrol and moved back to our checkpoint. I tried to have a drink from my water vessel that you carry inside your rucksack, but there was no water left in it. It was only when I took it off and looked at it, I realized it had three bullet holes through it - I felt so lucky!

An ambush is the worst situation for a soldier. Here, they are surrounded by the enemy, usually in an area with little cover. Friendly fire is another risk for a soldier. In the confusion of war, in darkness and smoke, soldiers can be killed by their own side in the crossfire.

UNDER ATTACK

In war, soldiers have to defend large bases as well as smaller observation posts and checkpoints. Bases are **fortified** and placed on terrain that gives the defensive side a big advantage.

The military build bases on high ground with good views all around. Any trees or buildings in the area are cleared away. **Sentry** guards keep a constant look out for enemy activity. Sometimes sentry towers are built on a base for stationing snipers.

▼ A firefight breaks out along the wall of an operating base in Afghanistan. Walls have to frequently be repaired as the insurgents blast holes in them with their rocket-propelled grenades.

Camouflage is the use of materials to disguise the appearance of military targets. It is used on troops, clothing, equipment, and vehicles.

"Our mission in Afghanistan was to take over a simple compound and set it up as a patrol base. The first time I got shot at in my life was when the helicopters dropped us off. Bullets were pinging off the helicopter. Inside the compound we were getting attacked from just 150 feet (45 m) away. Rocket-propelled grenades would come flying over the wall—it was down to luck if one landed by you. Over the course of a few weeks we extended the walls of our compound and forced the enemy back. CCTV cameras were installed to keep an eye on the enemy. Later on we launched a **blimp** a thousand feet (300 m) into the air to survey the area."

Captain Toby Whitmarsh

When facing an enemy using bombs and air power, troops defend their positions underground. Soldiers are trained to dig triangular-shaped trenches called harbors. Each side of the trench is guarded by a section of troops. Weeds and foliage are used to blend the harbor into the background.

▼ A U.S. soldier keeps watch at a checkpoint as mortar explosives hit a nearby mountainside.

BEHIND ENEMY LINES

Small units of the infantry are expert at gathering information about the enemy. These reconnaissance (recon) troops are highly trained in the art of **stealth** and can spend long periods of time close to, or behind enemy lines without being detected.

Reconnaissance missions involve small teams of three or four men. They report back on an enemy's set-up, their troop numbers and weapons, and potential targets that could be attacked or ambushed. They can even call in an **air strike** on a specific target. One of the team is expert at sketching and makes drawings of the area.

> " The job is physically taxing because you have to move long distances with a heavy load that supports you while on a mission. The ability to stay out of sight and to have the mental discipline not to move around during the day and be discovered is just as taxing as the physical stuff. "
>
> **Brendon E. Wellendorf, senior scout observer**

Recon troops are also sent out to evaluate terrain. They may be asked to find the safest route that troops can use to move forward. Recon is a vital part of warfare, but highly dangerous. Small teams run the risk of being overwhelmed if they are spotted. If they are not killed they could be taken as **hostages**.

The teams usually operate at night using devices such as night viewing goggles and **thermal imaging** weapon sights. They make the minimum amount of noise and are careful not to leave trails such as footprints and tire tracks. In the day, camouflage is crucial.

"When teams conduct a short halt, they will do what is called SLLS, stop, look, listen, and smell. During the halt it is important that the team remains completely still and silent so they can use their senses when observing the area."

Sergeant Christopher Brown

▲ Soldiers practice reconnaissance missions, testing their land navigation and survival skills.

RAIDS

Infantry soldiers are trained to raid enemy compounds and take out any threats. During a raid the fighting is the fastest and most intense a soldier will experience. Raids are carried out after a recon team has gathered intelligence. They might have reported that a building contains an important target or that a hostage is being held.

For the most important and deadly raids, the army can call in their special forces, such as the U.S. Army's Delta Force or the U.K.'s SAS. These elite fighters are masters at clearing a building by force.

▲ Soldiers storm a house suspected of holding terrorists.

First, troops approach their target with stealth. The first men then break into the building and secure the point of entry. They may blast the entry with explosives. Inside they throw stun grenades, which bang so loudly that they paralyze any enemies. Each room is cleared in order. While two men secure one room, two more men move on to clear the next room. Torches are used to check every single part of the building and a cordon of troops is placed around the compound to stop anyone escaping. With so much action in a short space of time troops must be careful that they do not kill innocent people or their own soldiers.

▼ Soldiers clear rooms one by one.

Captain Toby Whitmarsh of the British Army says that in Afghanistan the biggest threat is from **improvised explosive devices (IEDs)**:

> When we clear compounds there are often IEDs and other booby traps. The bravest man is the soldier who leads the way. He carries a metal detector with him to check for explosive devices. Men on ladders, armed with machine guns, look down from the windows to give him cover. He marks with chalk where he has been so the rest of us know where it is safe to go.

ON PATROL

When the troops leave their base to go out on their daily patrols danger lurks around every corner. During firefights rounds of bullets rain down on the patrol. There is the threat of an ambush or worse still treading on an explosive device.

"I am not scared of a firefight. They can shoot at me all day. But the IEDs you have no idea when it is going to come at you. You never have any idea when your time is up."

Corporal Andrew Bryant

▼ An armored fighting vehicle lies on its side after an IED buried in the ground explodes.

Patrols are conducted to keep guard over an area and assess the enemy's activity. The infantry's aim is to dominate the ground in front of their defensive positions and if necessary destroy the enemy. Patrols can be carried out with vehicles or on foot. The number of troops in a patrol depends on the threat level.

Soldiers on patrol keep spaces between each other. Then, if a missile or mortar drops down on them or an explosive is set off, it will only kill one or two men instead of the whole section. Patrols go out every day, but they must not be predictable. If they go over the same ground the enemy will know where to attack.

A patrol includes specialists of various weaponry including a sniper and a sharpshooter, who uses an accurate, long-range rifle. There is always a medic, and an air–and–mortar fire controller who relays orders back to base. Whenever a patrol stops, soldiers move into their fire positions. They must always be alert—a moment's loss of concentration can cost them their lives.

▲ Sending out patrols is a demonstration of force, but soldiers need to be alert to the dangers.

ESCORTING

The infantry escort and provide security to **convoys** of military and civilian vehicles. They face huge dangers when they protect other units from ambush.

Soldiers with a convoy must stay alert for hours at a time, scanning the roads and fields for possible threats. The mission's commander sits at the front with the driver and calls out suspicious obstacles or possible roadside bombs. Gunners keep watch from the tops of the vehicles. In a split second they must recognize the difference between an ordinary civilian and an enemy.

▼ A gunner scans nearby hills for threats to his convoy.

"I search and scan for a lot of things, small-arms, IEDs, and stuff like that. It's actually a stressful job up there because you're constantly looking for threats. It's all about staying vigilant and not getting complacent. What helps me stay focused is just doing the job, I have to keep in mind that it's not only me in the truck. Not only that but you have the entire convoy and you have to take care of each other. Being a gunner is a big responsibility because we are the trigger-pullers."

Sergeant Brandon J. Robertson, gunner

Convoy Escort Teams (CETs)

consist of soldiers that are hand-picked for their experience, professionalism, and responsible nature. CETs must know how to fix the vehicles as well as provide security so that the convoy does not get stuck on the road.

▲ A convoy presses ahead using a stream as a roadway.

CONSTRUCTION

The infantry constructs defenses, roads, bridges, airfields, and many other structures, which will give them an advantage on the battlefield. Soldiers doing building work are exposed and vulnerable to attack. A new military post or bridge can be a battle winner, so the enemy will be eager to stop it.

At war, soldiers are constantly in a process of fortifying and improving defenses, whether it is building walls or towers, or digging **shellscrapes** and trenches. Troops can spend whole days just digging. Trenches then need to be fortified with wood and have communications systems and sentry positions built in.

▶ With the help of a mechanical digger soldiers construct a trench system.

The engineers in the infantry have a flat-pack bridge that they can build in 40 minutes. The bridges are used to bypass enemy positions or roadblocks. They also build roads to make supply routes and connect checkpoints. Armored vehicles and riflemen provide the troops with cover as they work.

Corporal Damian Monks describes how he rushed to build a checkpoint in record time:

> "We were told that we needed to pull out all the stops to get it done in four days, but that just motivated us to get it done in three. The boys worked really hard, even in the midday heat, which made it very easy from my point of view. It was also good to know that the infantry boys from 5 Rifles had our backs so we could concentrate on the job in hand."

▶ A soldier keeps his weapon handy in case insurgents decide to disrupt his work.

ANTI-TERRORISM

Terrorists are people that use violence and threats to gain political control or attention. Since 2001, infantry soldiers from the U.S., Canada, the U.K., and many other countries have been fighting terror in Afghanistan.

Terrorist attacks come in deadly forms. Some terrorists choose to detonate a suicide bomb which kills themselves as well as those around them. The explosives are strapped to the bomber's chest or on a vehicle, which they ram into a building. The result is often carnage, with bodies and blood scattered across the ground.

▲ Insurgents are captured by the infantry in this role-playing exercise.

Fighting terror is especially dangerous because you cannot always be sure who the enemy is. The U.S. Army has a new radar system called CounterBomber, which from a safe distance can detect a bomb hidden underneath a person's clothing. Reconnaissance work is vital to gain information on terrorists' whereabouts and plans. Soldiers on patrol look out for any suspicious activity and question civilians. Many terrorists sell drugs to fund their activities. Raids are carried out to kill terrorists and find stashes of weapons and drugs.

> "If we have actionable intelligence about high-value terrorist targets and President Musharraf [former president of Pakistan] won't act, we will... There must be no safe haven for terrorists who threaten America. We cannot fail to act because action is hard."
>
> **Barack Obama, President of the United States**

▼ Fifteen million dollars worth of drugs are recovered in Kandahar, Afghanistan, after a U.S. Army investigation.

KEEPING THE PEACE

After a war is won, the infantry must stay and create the conditions for a long-lasting peace. Peacekeeping missions are ongoing in countries all over the world. They can be just as stressful and dangerous as all-out war.

In the aftermath of war, troops need to protect the process of rebuilding schools and hospitals, too. These buildings are highly vulnerable as terrorists do not want the army to be seen doing positive things for the local people.

▲ A member of a Female Engagement Team (FET) greets Afghan children. The team was sent to Afghanistan to engage with the local community.

◄ U.S. soldiers train local forces so that they can defend themselves from insurgents.

Soldiers may keep the peace while a country holds **elections** and sets up a government. The troops may also help to train a police force and army for the country. During this time the threat of an attack from warring opponents is high. Soldiers guard important buildings and ensure that aid, such as food packages, get safely through to people.

In Afghanistan troops are trying to rebuild the country and repel the insurgents at the same time. Captain Toby Whitmarsh says that the conflict is now about winning the support of the locals:

"Instead of fighting for position we are fighting to convince the locals that we are the better alternative to the insurgents. We chat to the locals, find out their concerns and what they need to make their lives easier. At the same time we must be careful who we are talking to and not leak any vital information that would put us in danger."

"The locals really do like us being here—they tell us that because the insurgents are running scared from us and the Afghan forces in their area, they can now go about their daily lives without being threatened or beaten up."

Terry Brazier, gunner

IT'S A FACT!

The U.S. Army has over 200,000 troops posted overseas, with a presence in more than 130 countries, covering every time zone. It has 13 military bases in countries around Afghanistan.

A grenade launcher is usually attached underneath the barrel of a rifle. The M203 grenade launcher is designed to take out doors, windows, bunkers, and some light armored vehicles. It can fire a total of ten different rounds. The various rounds include a highly explosive one intended to kill groups of enemy combatants, a white star cluster used for illuminating battlefields and enemy targets, and a sponge grenade that is non-lethal and used for crowd control.

The number of U.S. troops that died in the war in Iraq from 2003 to 2011 totalled 4,486. 54 percent of the casualties were under 25 years old. The number of troops wounded during the war was 32,226.

Terrorists have been known to take hostages aboard trains, buses, and coaches. Special forces train constantly in assaulting such targets. S.A.S. training facilities include a stretch of railway tracks complete with railway carriages where they practice storming hijacked trains. Only one in 12 candidates make it through the S.A.S.'s gruelling selection process.

All of the combat necessities such as ammunition, weapon systems, food and clothing, and shelter are carried on the backs of the infantry. Loads of 80 pounds (36 kg) are common and greater loads in excess of 100 pounds (45 kg) are not unheard of.

Some countries allow women to fill active combat roles in the infantry, such as Australia, Canada, and France. The U.S. and U.K. military do not.

Infantry Soldiers Online
www.goarmy.com
www.army.mil
www.army.mod.uk

GLOSSARY

air strike An attack made by aircraft

ambush A surprise attack by people lying in wait

artillery Large guns that fire rockets and bombs and are usually transported on a wheeled carriage

bayonet A blade fixed to a rifle for use in hand-to-hand combat

blimp A small airship

checkpoint A manned barrier where security checks are carried out

convoy A group of vehicles traveling together

election The choice of a government by a public vote

engineer A person who designs and builds machines or structures

flank The right or left side of an army's formation

formation The pattern that soldiers position themselves in

fortified Strengthened a place's defenses to protect it against attack

hostage A person who is held prisoner by captors

improvised explosive device (IED) A homemade bomb which can be triggered by pressure, a trip wire, or remote control

insurgent A person who rises up against the government

intelligence Information collected by the military which is of strategic value

mine A bomb placed just below the surface of the ground

mortar A gun for firing bombs from a long distance

navigation Planning and following a route

nuclear Describes something that uses the energy gained from splitting atoms

reconnaissance Observation of an area to locate an enemy or gain strategic information

sentry A soldier stationed to keep guard

shellscrape A shallow hole in the earth that a soldier can lie down and take cover in

stealth Action that is done with caution and secrecy

thermal imaging A technique where the heat given off by an object is used to produce an image of it

INDEX